Primer Catecismo

First Catechism

Spanish/English Parallel Edition
Edición Paralela Español/Inglés

GREAT COMMISSION
PUBLICATIONS

First Catechism (English Text) © 2003 by Great Commission Publications
ISBN 978-0-934688-68-0

Spanish/English Parallel Edition © 2020 by Great Commission Publications
ISBN 978-1-7320823-2-8
1st Printing, 2020
Printed in the United States of America

Scripture quotations are Proverbs 8:17, Psalm 7:11, Exodus 20:3–17, Matthew 6:9–13
and Matthew 19:14 from the following versions: New King James Version (NKJV),
copyright © 1982 by Thomas Nelson, Inc., used by permission; King James Version (KJV);
and New International Version (NIV), copyright © 1973, 1978, 1984,
The International Bible Society, used by permission of Zondervan Bible Publishers.

Las citas bíblicas en español han sido tomado de la Reina-Valera © 1960 Sociedades
Bíblicas en América Latina (RVR 1960); © renovado 1988 por Sociedades Bíblicas Unidas.
Utilizado con permiso. Reina-Valera 1960™ es una marca registrada de la Sociedad Bíblica
Americana, y puede ser usada solamente bajo licencia. Otras citas bíblicas han sido tomado
de la Santa Biblia, Nueva Versión Internacional® NVI® © 1999, 2015 por Bíblica, Inc.®
Usado con permiso de Bíblica, Inc.® Reservados todos los derechos en todo el mundo.

Spanish Translation by David W. Robertson
Language Review by Sandra Kunkel and Zury Jennings
Edited by Miriam Selle Nazario
Graphic Design by Isa Mohtaj

Great Commission Publications is the joint publishing ministry
of the Orthodox Presbyterian Church and the Presbyterian Church in America.

Great Commission Publications es el ministerio de publicación conjunta de
la Iglesia Presbiteriana Ortodoxa y la Iglesia Presbiteriana en América.

GREAT COMMISSION
PUBLICATIONS

3640 Windsor Park Drive · Suwanee, GA 30024
www.gcp.org · 800-695-3387

Let the word of Christ dwell in you richly,
teaching and admonishing one another in all wisdom,
singing psalms and hymns and spiritual songs, with
thankfulness in your hearts to God. COLOSSIANS 3:16

Que habite en ustedes la palabra de Cristo con toda
su riqueza: instrúyanse y aconséjense unos a otros con
toda sabiduría; canten salmos, himnos y canciones
espirituales a Dios, con gratitud de corazón. COLOSENSES 3:16

PREFACIO

El Catequizar—la instrucción sistemática utilizando preguntas y respuestas sencillas—es una herramienta comprobada y efectiva para la enseñanza de las verdades bíblicas. *Primer Catecismo* se presenta a los aprendices un vocabulario de fe y de las doctrinas de la gracia. Debe ser visto como un escalón para un estudio posterior del Catecismo Menor de Westminster.

Primer Catecismo es un manual práctico de la fe cristiana. Esta adaptación está basada en un catecismo publicado por Joseph P. Engels en 1840. *Primer Catecismo* presenta y simplifica los conceptos del Catecismo Menor, una parte de los Estándares de Westminster. Cambios en el vocabulario, la gramática y la secuencia de las preguntas hacen más claro y accesible el catecismo.

Esta edición presenta el texto en español en las páginas al lado izquierdo y el texto inglés en las páginas al lado derecho.

PREFACE

Catechizing—systematic instruction using simple questions and answers—is a tried and effective tool for the teaching of biblical truths. *First Catechism* introduces learners to a vocabulary of faith and the doctrines of grace. It should be regarded as a steppingstone for later study of the Westminster Shorter Catechism.

First Catechism is a primer on the Christian faith. This adaptation is based on a catechism published by Joseph P. Engels in 1840. It introduces and simplifies the concepts of the Shorter Catechism, one part of the Westminster Standards. Changes in vocabulary, grammar, and the sequence of questions make the catechism clearer and more accessible.

This edition features Spanish text on the left-hand pages and English text on the right-hand pages.

Primer Catecismo

1 **P. ¿Quién te creó?**
   R. Dios.

2 **P. ¿Qué más creó Dios?**
   R. Dios creó todas las cosas.

3 **P. ¿Para qué te creó Dios,
   y para que creó todas las cosas?**
   R. Para su propia gloria.

4 **P. ¿Cómo puedes glorificar a Dios?**
   R. Amándolo y haciendo lo que él manda.

5 **P. ¿Por qué debes glorificar a Dios?**
   R. Porque él me creó y me cuida.

6 **P. ¿Hay más de un Dios verdadero?**
   R. No. Solo hay un Dios verdadero.

7 **P. ¿En cuántas personas existe
   este único Dios?**
   R. En tres personas.

First Catechism

1 Q. Who made you?
A. God.

2 Q. What else did God make?
A. God made all things.

3 Q. Why did God make you and all things?
A. For his own glory.

4 Q. How can you glorify God?
A. By loving him and doing what he commands.

5 Q. Why are you to glorify God?
A. Because he made me and takes care of me.

6 Q. Is there more than one true God?
A. No. There is only one true God.

7 Q. In how many Persons does this one God exist?
A. In three Persons.

8   **P.** **Menciona a estas tres Personas.**

     R. El Padre, el Hijo y el Espíritu Santo.

9   **P.** **¿Qué es Dios?**

     R. Dios es un Espíritu y no tiene cuerpo como los humanos.

10   **P.** **¿Dónde está Dios?**

     R. Dios está en todas partes.

11   **P.** **¿Puedes ver a Dios?**

     R. No. No puedo ver a Dios, pero él siempre me ve.

12   **P.** **¿Sabe Dios todas las cosas?**

     R. Sí. De Dios no se puede esconder nada.

13   **P.** **¿Puede Dios hacer todas las cosas?**

     R. Sí. Dios puede hacer toda su santa voluntad.

14   **P.** **¿Dónde aprendes a amar y obedecer a Dios?**

     R. Solamente en la Biblia.

Q. Name these three Persons.

A. The Father, the Son and the Holy Spirit.

Q. What is God?

A. God is a Spirit and does not have a body like men.

Q. Where is God?

A. God is everywhere.

Q. Can you see God?

A. No. I cannot see God, but he always sees me.

Q. Does God know all things?

A. Yes. Nothing can be hidden from God.

Q. Can God do all things?

A. Yes. God can do all his holy will.

Q. Where do you learn how to love and obey God?

A. In the Bible alone.

15

P. ¿Quiénes escribieron la Biblia?

R. Hombres elegidos que fueron inspirados por el Espíritu Santo.

16

P. ¿Quiénes fueron nuestros primeros padres?

R. Adán y Eva.

17

P. ¿Cómo creó Dios al hombre?

R. Dios creó al hombre, varón y hembra, a su propia imagen.

18

P. ¿Cómo fueron creados nuestros primeros padres?

R. Dios creó el cuerpo de Adán del polvo de la tierra, y el cuerpo de Eva de una costilla de Adán.

19

P. ¿Qué más les dio Dios a Adán y Eva además de cuerpos?

R. Les dio almas que vivirán para siempre.

20

P. ¿Tú también tienes un cuerpo y un alma?

R. Sí. Y mi alma va a vivir para siempre.

Q. Who wrote the Bible?

A. Chosen men who were inspired by the Holy Spirit.

Q. Who were our first parents?

A. Adam and Eve.

Q. How did God create man?

A. God created man, male and female, after his own image.

Q. Of what were our first parents made?

A. God made Adam's body out of the ground and Eve's body out of a rib from Adam.

Q. What else did God give Adam and Eve besides bodies?

A. He gave them souls that will last forever.

Q. Do you have a soul as well as a body?

A. Yes. And my soul is going to last forever.

21   **P.**   **¿Cómo sabes que tu alma vivirá para siempre?**

     R.   Porque así me lo dice la Biblia.

22   **P.**   **¿En qué condición creó Dios a Adán y Eva?**

     R.   Los creó santos y felices.

23   **P.**   **¿Qué pacto hizo Dios con Adán?**

     R.   El pacto de vida.

24   **P.**   **¿Qué es un pacto?**

     R.   Una relación que Dios establece con nosotros y que promete cumplir por su palabra.

25   **P.**   **En el pacto de vida, ¿qué le mandó Dios a Adán que hiciera?**

     R.   Que obedeciera perfectamente a Dios.

26   **P.**   **¿Qué prometió Dios en el pacto de vida?**

     R.   Recompensar a Adán con la vida si obedecía perfectamente a Dios.

Q. How do you know your soul will last forever?

A. Because the Bible tells me so.

Q. In what condition did God make Adam and Eve?

A. He made them holy and happy.

Q. What covenant did God make with Adam?

A. The covenant of life.

Q. What is a covenant?

A. A relationship that God establishes with us and guarantees by his word.

Q. In the covenant of life, what did God require Adam to do?

A. To obey God perfectly.

Q. What did God promise in the covenant of life?

A. To reward Adam with life if he obeyed God perfectly.

27 **P.** **¿Qué amenazó hacer Dios en el pacto de vida?**

R. Castigar a Adán con muerte si desobedecía a Dios.

28 **P.** **¿Cumplió Adán el pacto de vida?**

R. No. Él pecó contra Dios.

29 **P.** **¿Qué es el pecado?**

R. El pecado es cualquier falta de conformid a la ley de Dios, o la transgresión de ella.

30 **P.** **¿Qué quiere decir falta de conformidad**

R. No hacer o ser lo que Dios exige.

31 **P.** **¿Qué quiere decir transgresión?**

R. Hacer lo que Dios prohíbe.

32 **P.** **¿Qué merece todo pecado?**

R. La ira y la maldición de Dios.

33 **P.** **¿Cuál fue el pecado de nuestros primeros padres?**

R. Comer la fruta prohibida.

Q. **What did God threaten in the covenant of life?**

A. To punish Adam with death if he disobeyed God.

Q. **Did Adam keep the covenant of life?**

A. No. He sinned against God.

Q. **What is sin?**

A. Sin is any lack of conformity to, or transgression of, the law of God.

Q. **What is meant by lack of conformity?**

A. Not being or doing what God requires.

Q. **What is meant by transgression?**

A. Doing what God forbids.

Q. **What does every sin deserve?**

A. The wrath and curse of God.

Q. **What was the sin of our first parents?**

A. Eating the forbidden fruit.

34 **P.** **¿Quién tentó a Adán y a Eva a este pecado?**

R. Satanás tentó primero a Eva, y entonces la usó para tentar a Adán.

35 **P.** **¿Cómo cambiaron Adán y Eva cuando pecaron?**

R. En vez de ser santos y felices, se hicieron pecadores y miserables.

36 **P.** **¿Actuó Adán solamente para sí mismo en el, pacto de vida?**

R. No. El representó a la raza humana.

37 **P.** **¿Qué efecto tuvo el pecado de Adán en ti y en todos los humanos?**

R. Todos nacemos culpables y pecadores.

38 **P.** **¿Qué tan pecador eres por naturaleza?**

R. Soy corrupto en cada parte de mi ser.

39 **P.** **¿Cómo se llama la naturaleza pecadora que heredamos de Adán?**

R. Pecado original.

34 Q. **Who tempted Adam and Eve to this sin?**

A. Satan tempted Eve first, and then he used her to tempt Adam.

35 Q. **How did Adam and Eve change when they sinned?**

A. Instead of being holy and happy, they became sinful and miserable.

36 Q. **Did Adam act for himself alone in the covenant of life?**

A. No. He represented the whole human race.

37 Q. **What effect did the sin of Adam have on you and all people?**

A. We are all born guilty and sinful.

38 Q. **How sinful are you by nature?**

A. I am corrupt in every part of my being.

39 Q. **What is the sinful nature that we inherit from Adam called?**

A. Original sin.

40 P. ¿Puede ir al cielo cualquier persona con esta naturaleza pecadora?

R. No. Nuestros corazones tienen que ser cambiados antes de que podamos creer en Jesús e ir al cielo.

41 P. ¿Cómo se llama este cambio en el corazón?

R. El nuevo nacimiento, o regeneración.

42 P. ¿Quién puede cambiar el corazón de un pecador?

R. Sólo el Espíritu Santo.

43 P. ¿Puede ser salva cualquier persona a través del pacto de vida?

R. No. Nadie puede ser salvo por el pacto de vida.

44 P. Por qué nadie puede ser salvo por el pacto de vida?

R. Porque todos lo han rompido y son condenados por el mismo.

Q. **Can anyone go to heaven with this sinful nature?**

A. No. Our hearts must be changed before we can believe in Jesus and go to heaven.

Q. **What is this change of heart called?**

A. The new birth, or regeneration.

Q. **Who can change a sinner's heart?**

A. The Holy Spirit alone.

Q. **Can anyone be saved through the covenant of life?**

A. No. No one can be saved through the covenant of life.

Q. **Why can't anyone be saved through the covenant of life?**

A. Because all have broken it and are condemned by it.

45 **P. ¿Cómo rompiste tú el pacto de vida?**

R. Adán representó a todos, así que yo caí con Adán en su primer pecado.

46 **P. Entonces, ¿cómo puedes ser salvo?**

R. Por el Señor Jesucristo a través del pacto de gracia.

47 **P. ¿A quién representó Cristo en el pacto de gracia?**

R. A su pueblo elegido.

48 **P. ¿Cómo cumplió Cristo el pacto de gracia?**

R. Cristo obedeció la ley entera para su pueblo, y después sufrió el castigo merecido por los pecados de ellos.

49 **P. ¿Alguna vez pecó Jesús?**

R. No. Vivió una vida sin pecado.

50 **P. ¿Cómo podría sufrir Cristo?**

R. Cristo, el Hijo de Dios, se hizo hombre para poder obedecer la ley y sufrir en nuestro lugar.

45 **Q. How did you break the covenant of life?**

A. Adam represented all people, and so I fell with Adam in his first sin.

46 **Q. How, then, can you be saved?**

A. By the Lord Jesus Christ through the covenant of grace.

47 **Q. Whom did Christ represent in the covenant of grace?**

A. His elect people.

48 **Q. How did Christ fulfill the covenant of grace?**

A. Christ obeyed the whole law for his people, and then suffered the punishment due for their sins.

49 **Q. Did Jesus ever sin?**

A. No. He lived a sinless life.

50 **Q. How could Christ suffer?**

A. Christ, the Son of God, became a man so that he could obey and suffer in our place.

51   **P. ¿Por quiénes obedeció y sufrió Cristo?**

R. Por todos los que Dios el Padre le dio a Cristo.

52   **P. ¿Qué tipo de vida vivió Cristo en la tierra?**

R. Una vida de obediencia, servicio y sufrimiento.

53   **P. ¿Qué tipo de muerte sufrió Jesús?**

R. La dolorosa y vergonzosa muerte de la cruz.

54   **P. ¿Qué significa la expiación?**

R. Cristo satisfizo la justicia de Dios por su sufrimiento y muerte como substituto por los pecadores.

55   **P. ¿Qué garantiza Dios el Padre en el pacto de gracia?**

R. Justificar y santificar a todos aquellos por los cuales Cristo murió.

56   **P. ¿Cómo te justifica Dios?**

R. Dios perdona todos mis pecados y me acepta como justo por medio de Cristo.

Q. For whom did Christ obey and suffer?

A. For all whom God the Father gave to Christ.

Q. What kind of life did Christ live on earth?

A. A life of obedience, service and suffering.

Q. What kind of death did Jesus die?

A. The painful and shameful death of the cross.

Q. What is meant by the atonement?

A. Christ satisfied God's justice by his suffering and death as a substitute for sinners.

Q. What does God the Father guarantee in the covenant of grace?

A. To justify and sanctify all those for whom Christ died.

Q. How does God justify you?

A. God forgives all my sins and accepts me as righteous through Christ.

57 **P.** **¿Cómo te santifica Dios?**

R. Dios me hace cada vez más santo de corazón y comportamiento.

58 **P.** **¿Qué tienes que hacer para ser salvo?**

R. Tengo que arrepentirme de mi pecado y creer en Cristo como mi Salvador.

59 **P.** **¿Cómo te arrepientes de tu pecado?**

R. Tengo que lamentar mi pecado, aborrecerlo y abandonarlo.

60 **P.** **¿Por qué tienes que aborrecer y abandonar tu pecado?**

R. Porque el pecado desagrada a Dios.

61 **P.** **¿Qué significa creer en Cristo?**

R. Confiar solamente en Cristo para mi salvación.

62 **P.** **¿Puedes arrepentirte y creer en Cristo por tus propias fuerzas?**

R. No. No puedo arrepentirme ni creer a menos que el Espíritu Santo cambie mi corazón.

Q. How does God sanctify you?

A. God makes me more and more holy in heart and conduct.

Q. What must you do to be saved?

A. I must repent of my sin and believe in Christ as my Savior.

Q. How do you repent of your sin?

A. I must be sorry for my sin, and hate and forsake it.

Q. Why must you hate and forsake your sin?

A. Because sin displeases God.

Q. What does it mean to believe in Christ?

A. To trust in Christ alone for my salvation.

Q. Can you repent and believe in Christ by your own power?

A. No. I cannot repent and believe unless the Holy Spirit changes my heart.

63 **P. ¿Cómo puedes tener la ayuda del Espíritu Santo?**

R. Dios nos ha dicho que oremos para tener la ayuda del Espíritu Santo.

64 **P. ¿Hace cuánto tiempo murió Cristo?**

R. Hace unos dos mil años.

65 **P. ¿Cómo fueron salvos los pecadores antes de que viniera Cristo?**

R. Por creer en el Mesías prometido.

66 **P. Antes de que viniera Cristo, ¿cómo mostraron su fe los creyentes?**

R. Ofreciendo los sacrificios que Dios exigía.

67 **P. ¿Qué representaban esos sacrificios?**

R. Representaban a Cristo, el Cordero de Dios, que vendría para morir por los pecadores.

68 **P. ¿Cuántos oficios cumple Cristo como el Mesías prometido?**

R. Cristo cumple tres oficios.

Q. How can you get the help of the Holy Spirit?

A. God has told us to pray for the Holy Spirit's help.

Q. How long ago did Christ die?

A. About two thousand years ago.

Q. How were sinners saved before Christ came?

A. By believing in the promised Messiah.

Q. Before Christ came, how did believers show their faith?

A. By offering the sacrifices God required.

Q. What did these sacrifices represent?

A. Christ, the Lamb of God, who would come to die for sinners.

Q. How many offices does Christ fulfill as the promised Messiah?

A. Christ fulfills three offices.

69 **P. ¿Cuáles son?**

R. Los oficios de un profeta,
un sacerdote, y un rey.

70 **P. ¿Cómo es Cristo tu profeta?**

R. Cristo me enseña la voluntad de Dios.

71 **P. ¿Cómo es Cristo tu sacerdote?**

R. Cristo murió por mis pecados,
y sigue orando por mí.

72 **P. ¿Cómo es Cristo tu rey?**

R. Cristo reina sobre mí, el mundo y
Satanás, y también me defiende.

73 **P. ¿Por qué necesitas a Cristo
como tu profeta?**

R. Porque soy ignorante por naturaleza.

74 **P. ¿Por qué necesitas a Cristo
como tu sacerdote?**

R. Porque soy culpable de transgredir
la ley de Dios.

69 Q. What are they?

A. The offices of a prophet, of a priest, and of a king.

70 Q. How is Christ your prophet?

A. Christ teaches me the will of God.

71 Q. How is Christ your priest?

A. Christ died for my sins, and continues to pray for me.

72 Q. How is Christ your king?

A. Christ rules over me, the world and Satan, and he defends me.

73 Q. Why do you need Christ as your prophet?

A. Because I am ignorant by nature.

74 Q. Why do you need Christ as your priest?

A. Because I am guilty of breaking God's law.

75 P. ¿Por qué necesitas a Cristo como tu rey?

R. Porque soy débil e indefenso.

76 P. ¿Cuántos mandamientos dio Dios en el Monte Sinaí?

R. Diez mandamientos.

77 P. ¿Por qué debemos obedecer los Diez Mandamientos?

R. Porque Dios es nuestro Creador, Salvador y Rey.

78 P. ¿Qué enseñan los primeros cuatro mandamientos?

R. Lo que significa amar y servir a Dios.

79 P. ¿Qué enseñan los últimos seis mandamientos?

R. Lo que significa amar y servir a mi prójimo

80 P. ¿Qué enseñan los Diez Mandamientos?

R. Me enseñan a amar a Dios con todo mi corazón, y a mi prójimo como a mí mismo.

Q. Why do you need Christ as your king?

A. Because I am weak and helpless.

Q. How many commandments did God give on Mount Sinai?

A. Ten commandments.

Q. Why should we obey the Ten Commandments?

A. Because God is our Creator, Savior and King.

Q. What do the first four commandments teach?

A. What it means to love and serve God.

Q. What do the last six commandments teach?

A. What it means to love and serve my neighbor.

Q. What do the Ten Commandments teach?

A. To love God with all my heart, and my neighbor as myself.

81 **P. ¿Quién es tu prójimo?**

R. Cada persona es mi prójimo.

82 **P. ¿A Dios le agradan las personas que lo aman y obedecen?**

R. Sí. Dios dice, "Yo amo a los que me aman." (RVR 1960)

83 **P. ¿A Dios le desagradan las personas que no lo aman ni obedecen?**

R. Sí. "Dios está enojado con los malvados todos los días." (RVR 1960)

84 **P. ¿Cuál es el primer mandamiento?**

R. El primer mandamiento es "No tendrás dioses ajenos delante de mí." (RVR 1960)

85 **P. ¿Qué te enseña el primer mandamiento?**

R. Me enseña a adorar al Dios verdadero, y a él solamente.

81 Q. Who is your neighbor?

A. Everybody is my neighbor.

82 Q. Is God pleased with those who love and obey him?

A. Yes. God says, "I love them that love me." (KJV)

83 Q. Is God displeased with those who do not love and obey him?

A. Yes. "God is angry with the wicked every day." (KJV)

84 Q. What is the first commandment?

A. The first commandment is "You shall have no other gods before Me." (NKJV)

85 Q. What does the first commandment teach you?

A. To worship the true God, and him only.

86 **P. ¿Cuál es el segundo mandamiento?**

R. El segundo mandamiento es "No te hará imagen, ni ninguna semejanza de lo que esté arriba en el cielo, ni abajo en la tierr ni en las aguas debajo de la tierra. No te inclinarás a ellas, ni las honrarás; porque yo soy Jehová tu Dios, fuerte, celoso, que visito la maldad de los padres sobre los hijos hasta la tercera y cuarta generación c los que me aborrecen, y hago misericordi a millares, a los que me aman y guardan mis mandamientos." (RVR 1960)

87 **P. ¿Qué te enseña el segundo mandamiento**

R. Me enseña a adorar a Dios solamente como él manda, y a no adorar a Dios usando estatuas o imágenes.

88 **P. ¿Cuál es el tercer mandamiento?**

R. El tercer mandamiento es "No tomarás e nombre de Jehová tu Dios en vano; porqu no dará por inocente Jehová al que tomar su nombre en vano." (RVR 1960)

Q. What is the second commandment?

A. The second commandment is "You shall not make for yourself a carved image—any likeness of anything that is in heaven above, or that is in the earth beneath, or that is in the water under the earth; you shall not bow down to them nor serve them. For I, the LORD your God, am a jealous God, visiting the iniquity of the fathers upon the children to the third and fourth generations of those who hate Me, but showing mercy to thousands, to those who love Me and keep My commandments." (NKJV)

Q. What does the second commandment teach you?

A. To worship God only as he commands, and not to worship God by using statues or pictures.

Q. What is the third commandment?

A. The third commandment is "You shall not take the name of the LORD your God in vain, for the LORD will not hold him guiltless who takes His name in vain." (NKJV)

89 **P.** **¿Qué te enseña el tercer mandamiento?**

R. Me enseña a tratar con reverencia el nombre, la palabra y las obras de Dios.

90 **P.** **¿Cuál es el cuarto mandamiento?**

R. El cuarto mandamiento es "Acuérdate del día de reposo para santificarlo. Seis días trabajarás, y harás toda tu obra; mas el séptimo día es reposo para Jehová tu Dios; no hagas en él obra alguna, tú, ni tu hijo, ni tu hija, ni tu siervo, ni tu criada, ni tu bestia, ni tu extranjero que está dentro de tus puertas. Porque en seis días hizo Jehová los cielos y la tierra, el mar, y todas las cosas que en ellos hay, y reposó en el séptimo día; por tanto, Jehová bendijo el día de reposo y lo santificó." (RVR 1960)

91 **P.** **¿Qué te enseña el cuarto mandamiento?**

R. Me enseña a trabajar seis días y guardar como santo el día de reposo.

89 Q. What does the third commandment teach you?

A. To treat God's name, word and works with reverence.

90 Q. What is the fourth commandment?

A. The fourth commandment is "Remember the Sabbath day, to keep it holy. Six days you shall labor and do all your work, but the seventh day is the Sabbath of the LORD your God. In it you shall do no work: you, nor your son, nor your daughter, nor your male servant, nor your female servant, nor your cattle, nor your stranger who is within your gates. For in six days the LORD made the heavens and the earth, the sea, and all that is in them, and rested the seventh day. Therefore the LORD blessed the Sabbath day and hallowed it." (NKJV)

91 Q. What does the fourth commandment teach you?

A. To work six days and keep the Sabbath day holy.

92 **P. ¿Qué día de la semana es el día de reposo cristiano?**

R. El domingo, el primer día de la semana, llamado el Día del Señor.

93 **P. ¿Por qué se llama el Día del Señor?**

R. Porque en ese día el Señor Jesús resucitó de los muertos.

94 **P. ¿Cómo debes guardar el Día del Señor?**

R. Debo descansar de mi trabajo diario y adorar fielmente a Dios.

95 **P. ¿Cuál es el quinto mandamiento?**

R. El quinto mandamiento es "Honra a tu padre y a tu madre, para que tus días se alarguen en la tierra que Jehová tu Dios te da." (RVR 1960)

96 **P. ¿Qué te enseña el quinto mandamiento?**

R. Me enseña a amar y a obedecer a mis padres y a todos aquellos que Dios designe sobre mí.

Q. What day of the week is the Christian Sabbath?

A. The first day of the week, called the Lord's Day.

Q. Why is it called the Lord's Day?

A. Because on that day the Lord Jesus Christ rose from the dead.

Q. How should you keep the Lord's Day?

A. I should rest from my daily work and faithfully worship God.

Q. What is the fifth commandment?

A. The fifth commandment is "Honor your father and your mother, that your days may be long upon the land which the LORD your God is giving you." (NKJV)

Q. What does the fifth commandment teach you?

A. To love and obey my parents and all others that God appoints over me.

97 **P.** **¿Cuál es el sexto mandamiento?**

R. El sexto mandamiento es "No matarás." (RVR 1960)

98 **P.** **¿Qué te enseña el sexto mandamiento?**

R. Me enseña a no quitar la vida de nadie injustamente, y a no pecar cuando estoy enojado.

99 **P.** **¿Cuál es el séptimo mandamiento?**

R. El séptimo mandamiento es "No cometerás adulterio." (RVR 1960)

100 **P.** **¿Qué te enseña el séptimo mandamiento?**

R. Me enseña a ser puro del corazón, lenguaje y conducta, y a ser fiel en el matrimonio.

101 **P.** **¿Cuál es el octavo mandamiento?**

R. El octavo mandamiento es "No hurtarás." (RVR 1960)

Q. What is the sixth commandment?

A. The sixth commandment is "You shall not murder." (NKJV)

Q. What does the sixth commandment teach you?

A. Not to take anyone's life unjustly and not to sin when I am angry.

Q. What is the seventh commandment?

A. The seventh commandment is "You shall not commit adultery." (NKJV)

Q. What does the seventh commandment teach you?

A. To be pure in heart, language and conduct, and to be faithful in marriage.

Q. What is the eighth commandment?

A. The eighth commandment is "You shall not steal." (NKJV)

102 P. **¿Qué te enseña el octavo mandamiento**

R. Me enseña a no tomar nada que le pertenezca a alguien más.

103 P. **¿Cuál es el noveno mandamiento?**

R. El noveno mandamiento es "No hablarás contra tu prójimo falso testimonio." (RVR 196

104 P. **¿Qué te enseña el noveno mandamiento?**

R. Me enseña a jamás mentir, sino decir la verdad en todo tiempo.

105 P. **¿Cuál es el décimo mandamiento?**

R. El décimo mandamiento es "No codiciar la casa de tu prójimo, no codiciarás la mujer de tu prójimo, ni su siervo, ni su criada, ni su buey, ni su asno, ni cosa alguna de tu prójimo." (RVR 1960)

106 P. **¿Qué te enseña el décimo mandamiento?**

R. Me enseña a estar contento con lo que Dios elija darme.

Q. **What does the eighth commandment teach you?**

A. Not to take anything that belongs to someone else.

Q. **What is the ninth commandment?**

A. The ninth commandment is "You shall not bear false witness against your neighbor." (NKJV)

Q. **What does the ninth commandment teach you?**

A. Never to lie, but to tell the truth at all times.

Q. **What is the tenth commandment?**

A. The tenth commandment is "You shall not covet your neighbor's house; you shall not covet your neighbor's wife, nor his male servant, nor his female servant, nor his ox, nor his donkey, nor anything that is your neighbor's." (NKJV)

Q. **What does the tenth commandment teach you?**

A. To be content with whatever God chooses to give me.

107 P. ¿Puedes guardar perfectamente los Diez Mandamientos?

R. No. Desde la caída de Adán, el único que ha podido hacer esto es Jesús.

108 P. ¿De qué te sirven los Diez Mandamientos?

R. Me enseñan lo que le agrada a Dios, y cuánto necesito a un Salvador.

109 P. ¿Qué es la oración?

R. La oración es alabar a Dios, dar gracias por sus bendiciones, y pedirle las cosas que él ha prometido en la Biblia.

110 P. ¿En el nombre de quién debemos orar?

R. Sólo en el nombre de Cristo.

111 P. ¿Qué nos dio Cristo para enseñarnos cómo orar?

R. La oración "El Padre Nuestro."

**107 Q. Can you keep the
Ten Commandments perfectly?**

A. No. Since the fall of Adam,
the only One who has been
able to do this is Jesus.

**108 Q. Of what use are the
Ten Commandments to you?**

A. They teach me what is pleasing to
God, and how much I need a Savior.

109 Q. What is prayer?

A. Prayer is praising God, giving thanks
for all his blessings, and asking him for
the things he has promised in the Bible.

110 Q. In whose name should we pray?

A. Only in the name of Christ.

**111 Q. What did Christ give us to
teach us about prayer?**

A. The Lord's Prayer.

112 P. **¿Qué dice el Padre Nuestro?**

R. El Padre Nuestro dice, "Padre Nuestro que estás en los cielos, santificado sea tu nombre. Venga tu Reino. Hágase tu voluntad, como en el cielo, así también en la tierra. El pan nuestro de cada día dánoslo hoy. Y perdónanos nuestras deudas, como también nosotros perdonamos a nuestros deudores. Y no nos metas en tentación, mas líbranos del mal; porque tuyo es el reino, y el poder, y la gloria, por todos los siglos. Amén." (RVR 1960)

113 P. **¿Cuántas peticiones hay en el Padre Nuestro?**

R. Seis.

114 P. **¿Cuál es la primera petición?**

R. La primera petición es "Santificado sea tu nombre."

115 P. **¿Qué significa orar, "Santificado sea tu nombre"?**

R. Estamos pidiéndole a Dios que nos ayude a nosotros y a los demás a respetarlo y honrarlo.

112 Q. What is the Lord's Prayer?

A. The Lord's Prayer is "Our Father which art in heaven, Hallowed be thy name. Thy kingdom come. Thy will be done in earth, as it is in heaven. Give us this day our daily bread. And forgive us our debts, as we forgive our debtors. And lead us not into temptation, but deliver us from evil: For thine is the kingdom, and the power, and the glory, for ever. Amen." (KJV)

113 Q. How many petitions are there in the Lord's Prayer?

A. Six.

114 Q. What is the first petition?

A. The first petition is "Hallowed be thy name."

115 Q. What does it mean to pray, "Hallowed be thy name"?

A. We are asking God to help us and others to respect and honor him.

116 P. ¿Cuál es la segunda petición?

R. La segunda petición es "Venga tu reino."

117 P. ¿Qué significa orar, "Venga tu reino"?

R. Estamos pidiéndole a Dios que traiga cada vez más y más personas para que oigan, crean, y obedezcan su evangelio.

118 P. ¿Cuál es la tercera petición?

R. La tercera petición es "Hágase tu voluntad como en el cielo, así también en la tierra."

119 P. ¿Qué significa orar, "Hágase tu voluntad, como en el cielo, así también en la tierra"?

R. Estamos pidiéndole a Dios que nos haga capaces y dispuestos a servirle en la tierra tal como él es servido en el cielo.

120 P. ¿Cuál es la cuarta petición?

R. La cuarta petición es "El pan nuestro de cada día dánoslo hoy."

16 **Q. What is the second petition?**

A. The second petition is "Thy kingdom come."

17 **Q. What does it mean to pray, "Thy kingdom come"?**

A. We are asking God to bring more and more people to hear, believe and obey his gospel.

18 **Q. What is the third petition?**

A. The third petition is "Thy will be done in earth, as it is in heaven."

19 **Q. What does it mean to pray, "Thy will be done in earth, as it is in heaven"?**

A. We are asking God to make us able and willing to serve him on earth just as he is served in heaven.

20 **Q. What is the fourth petition?**

A. The fourth petition is "Give us this day our daily bread."

121 P. ¿Qué significa orar "El pan nuestro de cada día dánoslo hoy"?

R. Estamos pidiéndole a Dios que nos provea todo lo que realmente necesitamos.

122 P. ¿Cuál es la quinta petición?

R. La quinta petición es "Y perdónanos nuestras deudas, como también nosotros perdonamos a nuestros deudores."

123 P. ¿Qué significa orar "Y perdónanos nuestras deudas, como también nosotros perdonamos a nuestros deudores"?

R. Estamos pidiéndole a Dios que perdone nuestros pecados por el amor de Cristo, y que nos capacite a perdonar a los demás

124 P. ¿Cuál es la sexta petición?

R. La sexta petición es "Y no nos metas en tentación, mas líbranos del mal."

21 **Q. What does it mean to pray, "Give us this day our daily bread"?**

A. We are asking God to provide us with all that we really need.

22 **Q. What is the fifth petition?**

A. The fifth petition is "And forgive us our debts, as we forgive our debtors."

23 **Q. What does it mean to pray, "And forgive us our debts, as we forgive our debtors"?**

A. We are asking God to forgive our sins for Christ's sake, and to make us willing to forgive others.

24 **Q. What is the sixth petition?**

A. The sixth petition is "And lead us not into temptation, but deliver us from evil."

125 P. ¿Qué significa orar, "Y no nos metas en tentación, mas líbranos del mal"?

R. Estamos pidiéndole a Dios que impida que seamos tentados, y que nos haga lo suficientemente fuertes para resistir la tentación.

126 P. ¿Cuántos sacramentos hay?

R. Dos.

127 P. ¿Cuáles son?

R. El Bautismo y la Santa Cena.

128 P. ¿Quién ordenó estos sacramentos?

R. El Señor Jesucristo.

129 P. ¿Para qué ordenó Cristo estos sacramentos?

R. Para distinguir a su pueblo del mundo, para consolarlos y fortalecerlos.

130 P. ¿Qué signo se utiliza en el bautismo?

R. El lavamiento con agua.

25 Q. What does it mean to pray, "And lead us not into temptation, but deliver us from evil"?

A. We are asking God to keep us from being tempted and to make us strong enough to resist when we are tempted.

26 Q. How many sacraments are there?

A. Two.

27 Q. What are they?

A. Baptism and the Lord's Supper.

28 Q. Who appointed these sacraments?

A. The Lord Jesus Christ.

29 Q. Why did Christ appoint these sacraments?

A. To distinguish his people from the world, and to comfort and strengthen them.

30 Q. What sign is used in baptism?

A. Washing with water.

131 P. ¿Qué representa el lavamiento con agua?

R. Que estamos unidos con Cristo y limpios del pecado, por medio de su sangre.

132 P. ¿En el nombre de quién somos bautizados?

R. En el nombre del Padre, del Hijo y del Espíritu Santo.

133 P. ¿Quiénes deben ser bautizados?

R. Los creyentes y sus hijos.

134 P. ¿Por qué somos bautizados aún como infantes pequeños?

R. Porque Dios incluye a los hijos de los creyentes en su pacto y los marca en el bautismo.

135 P. ¿Qué dijo Jesús sobre los niños?

R. "Dejen que los niños vengan a mí, y no se lo impidan, porque el reino de los cielos es de quienes son como ellos." (NVI)

31 Q. What does this washing with water represent?

A. That we are united to Christ and cleansed from sin by his blood.

32 Q. Into whose name are we baptized?

A. Into the name of the Father, and of the Son and of the Holy Spirit.

33 Q. Who are to be baptized?

A. Believers and their children.

34 Q. Why are we baptized even as little infants?

A. Because God includes the children of believers in his covenant and marks them in baptism.

35 Q. What did Jesus say about little children?

A. "Let the little children come to me, and do not hinder them, for the kingdom of heaven belongs to such as these." (NIV)

136 P. ¿A qué te llama el bautismo?

R. Me llama a ser un verdadero seguidor de Cristo.

137 P. ¿Qué signo se utiliza en la Santa Cena?

R. El comer pan y beber vino para recordar el sufrimiento y la muerte de Jesús.

138 P. ¿Qué representa el pan?

R. El cuerpo de Cristo sacrificado por nuestros pecados.

139 P. ¿Qué representa el vino?

R. La sangre de Cristo derramada por nuestros pecados.

140 P. ¿Quiénes pueden participar correctamente de la Santa Cena?

R. Los que se arrepienten de sus pecados, confían en Cristo, viven una vida santa, y confiesan su fe ante la Iglesia.

141 P. ¿Se quedó en el sepulcro Cristo después de la Crucifixión?

R. No. Al tercer día después de su muerte, resucitó corporalmente del sepulcro.

36 Q. What does baptism call you to be?

A. A true follower of Christ.

37 Q. What sign is used in the Lord's Supper?

A. Eating bread and drinking wine to remember the suffering and death of Jesus.

38 Q. What does the bread represent?

A. Christ's body sacrificed for our sins.

39 Q. What does the wine represent?

A. Christ's blood shed for our sins.

40 Q. Who may rightly partake of the Lord's Supper?

A. Those who repent of their sins, trust in Christ, live a godly life, and profess their faith before the Church.

41 Q. Did Christ remain in the grave after his crucifixion?

A. No. He rose bodily from the grave on the third day after his death.

142 P. ¿Dónde está Cristo ahora?

R. En el cielo, gobernando su reino e intercediendo por nosotros.

143 P. ¿Vendrá otra vez el Señor Jesús?

R. ¡Sí! Él volverá para juzgar al mundo en el último día.

144 P. ¿Qué les pasa a los creyentes cuando mueren?

R. Nuestros cuerpos volverán al polvo y nuestras almas irán para estar con el Señor para siempre.

145 P. ¿Qué les pasa a los no creyentes cuando mueren?

R. Sus cuerpos también volverán al polvo, pero sus almas irán al infierno.

146 P. ¿Qué es el infierno?

R. El infierno es un lugar horrible, donde los no creyentes están separados de Dios para sufrir por sus pecados.

142 Q. Where is Christ now?

A. In heaven, ruling his kingdom and interceding for us.

143 Q. Will the Lord Jesus come again?

A. Yes! He will return to judge the world on the last day.

144 Q. What happens to believers when they die?

A. Our bodies will return to the dust and our souls will go to be with the Lord forever.

145 Q. What happens to unbelievers when they die?

A. Their bodies will return to dust also, but their souls will go to hell.

146 Q. What is hell?

A. Hell is an awful place, where unbelievers are separated from God to suffer for their sins.

147 P. ¿Serán resucitados los cuerpos de todos los muertos?

R. Sí. En el último día, algunos serán resucitados para vida eterna y otros para muerte eterna.

148 P. ¿Qué hará Dios a los no creyentes en el último día?

R. Los juzgará, y los condenará a castigo eterno en el lago de fuego, con Satanás y sus ángeles.

149 P. ¿Qué hará Dios para los creyentes el último día?

R. Les dará un hogar con Él en el cielo nuevo y la tierra nueva.

150 P. ¿Cómo será el cielo nuevo y la tierra nueva?

R. Un lugar glorioso y feliz, donde los salvos estarán para siempre con Jesús.

47 Q. Will the bodies of all the dead be raised again?

A. Yes. At the last day some will be raised to everlasting life and others to everlasting death.

48 Q. What will God do to unbelievers at the last day?

A. He will judge them, and condemn them to everlasting punishment in the lake of fire with Satan and his angels.

49 Q. What will God do for believers at the last day?

A. He will give them a home with him in the new heaven and the new earth.

50 Q. What will the new heaven and the new earth be like?

A. A glorious and happy place, where the saved will be with Jesus forever.